THE LITTLE BOOK OF CHAMPAGNE TIPS

A

THE LITTLE BOOK OF CHAMPAGNE TIPS

ANDREW LANGLEY

Absolute Press

First published in Great Britain in 2013 by
Absolute Press, an imprint of Bloomsbury Publishing Plc
Scarborough House, 29 James Street West
Bath BA1 2BT, England
Phone +44 (0)1225 316013 **Fax** +44 (0)1225 445836
E-mail info@absolutepress.co.uk
Web www.absolutepress.co.uk

A catalogue record of this book is available from the British Library
ISBN 13: 9781472903594
Printed and bound by Replika Press Pvt. Ltd., India

Bloomsbury Publishing Plc
50 Bedford Square, London WC1B 3DP | www.bloomsbury.com

Reprinted 2018

FSC www.fsc.org MIX Paper from responsible sources FSC® C016779

'My only regret in life is that I did not drink more Champagne.'

John Maynard Keynes (1883-1946), British economist

1

Champagne is a wine which bubbles when you pour it out.

But there are hundreds of other varieties of sparkling wine – some just as expensive, some much cheaper. Some bear comparison with the great fizz, some are dreadful. Fine sparklers are made all over the world, from Spain and South America to California and New Zealand. Try them out.

2

If you want champagne, **make sure it really is champagne.**

This is pretty easy to establish. By law (in most countries) a wine can only be called champagne if it is produced in the region of Champagne in France. So, if the label bears the words 'Champagne' and 'France', it's champagne. All others are sparkling wines.

3

Treat champagne (and other sparkling wines) gently.

Unopened bottles are in a fairly unstable state, as they contain a liquid artificially stuffed with carbon dioxide. This is dying to escape, creating a pressure higher than that in your car tyres. Champagne bottles are good and strong, but have been known to explode under the strain.

4

Store your sparkling wines somewhere cool, dark and a bit humid.

They should be protected from sunlight, and stored on their sides. This, and the humidity, are vital, because the corks must be kept moist to stop them shrinking. A constant temperature prevents pressure changes inside the bottles.

5

Sparkling wines should be served very cold. This is because the carbon dioxide which forms the bubbles is more soluble at low temperatures. The result is a cold wine with smaller bubbles which last longer. The optimum temperature is somewhere between 6 and 9°C.

6

Give sparkling wine at least three hours to chill slowly.

You can put it in the fridge or into a bucket of ice. In frosty weather, you could put it outside on the back doorstep. But avoid the temptation to pop a bottle of good champagne in the freezer. The fierce shock can damage the fizziness and the flavour disastrously.

7

Take unopened bottles out of the fridge if you're not going to drink them immediately. Champagne will deteriorate if left in a refrigerator for more than a week or two. The rattling of the fridge motor and the frequent opening of the door will cause vibrations, and the very dry cold air may cause the cork to shrink.

8

In a tearing hurry? **There's an express method of chilling wine.**

Half-fill a bucket with ice. Chuck in a cup of salt, add water to cover and stir (with a spoon, not bare hands, as it will quickly get very cold indeed). Push the bottle down into the slush and leave no longer than 15 minutes.

9

Grapes are a quick indication of quality. Real champagne is made exclusively from three grape varieties: Pinot Noir, Chardonnay and Pinot Meunier. So are most other high quality sparkling wines (and say so on the label). Therefore – roughly speaking – you can regard anything made from one or all of these vines as reliably good.

10

Here's another major

indication of quality to look out for on the label. A decent sparkling wine will advertise itself as being made by the 'Traditional Method' or 'Méthode Champenoise' – that is, the way they make it in Champagne. Any other process makes inferior bubbly.

11

Opening and pouring #1: foil and wire.

Champagne is easily excited, so avoid shaking or jarring it. Put the bottle on a firm surface. So it points at the ceiling not at other people. Strip off the foil covering. Place one hand, with a tea towel, on top of the cork. Locate the twist in the wire muzzle and unwind it (anti-clockwise). Remove the wire.

12

Opening and pouring #2: the cork.

Grip the cork through the towel with one hand. With the other, hold the bottle firmly. Now turn the bottle – not the cork – until you feel it loosen. Work the cork gently out. Aim for nothing louder than a gentle hiss as it emerges. Have a glass handy to catch any froth which might overflow.

13

Opening and pouring #3: a stuck stopper.

Occasionally, the cork won't budge. Try twisting it with the towel, or levering it with your thumbs. Alternatively, use a pair of pliers to grip and twist it (carefully, or you may tear the top off altogether). As a last resort, run warm water over the cork end of the bottle.

14

Opening and pouring #4: into the glass.

Wait a few seconds after the cork's out, to allow any 'bottle stink' to dissipate. Then pour slowly. Tilt each glass so that the wine slides down the side, rather than splashing at the bottom. This will prevent it from foaming up and possibly – horrors! – overflowing the glass.

15

Serve sparkling wine in tall narrow glasses.

There are two good reasons for this. One: the bubbles of CO_2 will take longer to dissipate in the narrow space. And two: the drinker has a longer opportunity to enjoy the sight of the bubbles rising to the surface, glinting as they go.

16

Detergents are death to fizz. They cause the bubbles to collapse, and quickly make sparkling wines flat. So **rinse your glasses thoroughly** after washing to get rid of all soap traces. (Fats and oils – from things like lipstick and olive oil – can have the same effect.)

17

How sweet or dry is your sparkling wine?

Champagne has this defined on the label – in French, of course. At the dry end are ‘Extra Brut’ and ‘Brut’. In the middle comes ‘Sec’ and ‘Demi-sec’, while at the sweet end is ‘Doux’. Wines from other countries usually bear these definitions in their own language.

18

What is vintage champagne?

Every so often in the region there is an exceptionally good grape harvest. So the grower may decide to produce a wine using only that year's vintage (with minor additions), and date the bottle accordingly. In other years, the wine will be made from a blend of several vintages, and will thus be non-vintage (NV).

19

Have your

glasses at room temperature when serving sparkling wine.

Some people are tempted to chill them with ice or in the fridge (much as sherry is served in Spain). Avoid this. If the bottle itself is at the correct temperature, the wine could end up over-chilled by the icy glass. This can inhibit the production of bubbles and the release of the bouquet.

20

When drinking sparkling wine,

keep the glass as still as possible. The more you agitate the wine, the quicker the bubbles will disperse. Swilling the wine around the glass in order to release the 'nose' is really for still varieties. This behaviour is known by the French as 'L'Ennemi Numero 1 du Champagne'. Swirl it very gently if you must.

21

Hold your wine glass by the base

between thumb and index finger, or at very least by the stem only. If you cup the bowl of the glass, the warmth from your hand will soon take the chill and the fizz out of the champagne.

22

Champagnes
and sparkling wines
go well with a surprising
– sometimes astonishing –
variety of foods.

They are far more robust and assertive than you might imagine. So be bold, and experiment with your own combinations, making use of the range of dryness and sweetness available.

23

The slight **sweetness of a demi-sec** makes it an **intriguing match for savoury food.**

Try it with foie gras, or Thai fried-rice dishes. Most amazing of all is the experience of drinking demi-sec (or something even sweeter) with a powerful and salty blue cheese such as Roquefort or Bleu d'Auvergne.

24

Famously, **seafood is the classic food pairing with a brut sparkling wine.**

Shellfish, from lobster and crevettes to oysters and scallops, are particularly suited to the tart freshness of a dry fizzy. So too is the huge range of Japanese food including sushi and deep-fried tempura.

25

A bit of a surprise combination:

sparkling wine and fried food. The bubbles cut through the slight oiliness of the food, and complement its saltiness. Fried mushrooms are especially good, their mallowy texture a pleasing contrast with the crispness of champagne. High quality fish and chips also go well.

26

Save half-full bottles of sparkling wine

for up to a week by re-sealing them.
With determination and cunning you may be able to re-insert the original cork. Failing this, use a specialist champagne stopper, with a lever which hooks a rubber ring under the bottle lip. In emergency, use cling wrap and a rubber band. Reject silver spoons.

27

How long will a champagne last?

Most non-vintage sparklers are released when they are ready to drink. They won't get any better with age (in fact they will slowly deteriorate). On the other hand, a fine vintage champagne can age happily for another twenty years (under the right conditions).

28

Most champagne cocktails are on the sweetish side. They tend to contain fruits, sugar and syrups. So **the sparkling wine you use should generally be a dry one,** to add some tanginess and contrast. Brut is fine in most cases, but for a sugar-heavy cocktail, try an extra brut.

29

There are hundreds of different **champagne cocktails,** but just one central rule. Always **pour in the sparkling wine last** – after all the other ingredients. This way, you avoid disturbing the bubbles by additional pouring and stirring, and preserve most of the fizz.

30

A good champagne cocktail is only as good as the wine in it. If you use the cheapest fizz, the end result will suffer – the poor taste will come through somehow. On the other hand, vintage champagne is wasted in a cocktail. So compromise and use a middle-priced sparkling wine of the highest quality you can find.

31

Here's the classic champagne cocktail. Put a sugar cube in the bottom of a champagne flute. Drop three dashes of Angostura bitters on the sugar, then add a measure of cognac. Garnish with a slice of orange and maybe a maraschino cherry. Top up with champagne or a good sparkling wine.

32

For a proper buck's fizz,

put a teaspoon of grenadine (or Grand Marnier) in the bottom of a champagne flute. Add fresh, strained, orange juice to one third up the glass, plus a dash of orange bitters if possible. Fill up with a brut champagne, taking care not to build a froth which might overflow. Drink immediately.

33

Black velvet is another classic cocktail, and a very simple one too. Just half-fill a glass with stout, then gently add champagne. Yet there's more to it. The stout should be a good one (try something other than Guinness, such as a nutty, dry porter), while the wine can be relatively cheap (as its flavour will be swamped anyway).

34

Named after a Slim Gaillard song, the

Atomic Cocktail

is suitably anarchic. Shake shots of vodka, brandy and oloroso sherry, with some ice, in a shaker. Strain the mixture into a cocktail glass and top up with a reasonably good sparkling wine. *Vout-o-roonie!* as the man would say.

35

The Bellini is a Venetian creation, and is named after a peachy colour used by the painter Giovanni Bellini. Peel, stone and purée a ripe peach. Transfer the purée over ice into four champagne glasses. Pour a sparkling wine over it – preferably an Italian prosecco.

36

How did

the French 75

get its name? Never mind: it's a great cocktail, and a nicely acerbic contrast to the traditionally sweeter concoctions. Shake up a shot of gin, the juice of half a lemon, a teaspoon of sugar and some ice. Pour into a champagne flute (with more ice) and fill up with bubbly, stirring gently.

37

Champagne and strawberries

go together like foie gras and trumpets. Here's the first of two drink recipes. Whizz up a punnet of washed and hulled strawberries, and push through a sieve into a bowl. Mix in a tablespoon of sugar and maybe a dash of balsamic vinegar. Transfer to a glass and fill up with prosecco (or champagne).

38

This is a simpler, yet more sophisticated (and definitely

more alcoholic) champagne/ strawberry mix.

Put the strawberries in a glass bowl and cover with cognac. Leave overnight in the fridge. Next day, pop a few strawberries in the bottom of each glass and pour in champagne to the top.

39

Cucumber and champagne works peculiarly well.

Grate a cucumber into a sieve, and squeeze its juice through into a jug. Add the juice of ½ lemon, a bunch of fresh, bruised, mint leaves and 100ml elderflower cordial. Leave to infuse for an hour in the fridge. Pour into flutes and top with champagne and more torn mint leaves.

40

Dry sparkling wine gives a citric bite to chicken. Sauté sliced fennel and leek with chopped mushrooms in butter. Cover with chicken stock and simmer for 5 minutes. In another pan, brown 2 chicken breasts and transfer to the sauce. Deglaze the pan with 2 glasses of bubbly, then add this to the rest with half a cup of double cream and continue simmering until the chicken is cooked through.

41

Poach figs in sparkling wine.

Slit the top of 12 figs and pop in butter and sugar, then poach very gently in half a bottle of brut bubbly for 15 minutes. Remove the figs. Beat and heat 3 egg yolks and sugar in a bain-marie, then fold in the poaching wine and beat to a froth. Serve figs and froth with a dab of ice cream.

42

Most fish deserves a champagne sauce.

Fry monkfish fillet chunks briefly in olive oil and remove. Then brown slices of peeled, cored eating apple in the same pan. After 5 minutes, add sparkling wine and a dollop of cream. Return the fish and heat it all through for a minute or two. Season and serve.

43

Transform fish and chips with a champagne batter. The bubbles make the batter lighter and crunchier than ever. In a bowl, put 100g (4oz) each of cornflour and plain flour, plus chopped dill, lemon zest and a pinch of salt. Then whisk in half a bottle of sparkling wine. Dredge fish fillets in flour and the batter, and deep-fry.

44

Plain **risotto** has the simplest of ingredients – rice, stock and cheese.

Sparkling wine adds another dimension.

Slowly soften a chopped onion in olive oil. Bung in 2 cups of Arborio rice, then 4 cups of prosecco. Cook gently for 10 minutes, stirring frequently. Add enough chicken stock to keep the rice moist until it's cooked. Stir in grated parmesan.

45

Champagne can even cope with

a heavyweight like

braised beef.

Soften chopped onion, carrot and celery in olive oil. In another pan, brown chunks of floured beef shin, then add to the veg. Deglaze the pan with 4 cups of bubbly to absorb the meaty gunge, and pour that into the mix. Pop in bay leaves and tomato purée and cook on a low heat for 3 hours.

46

Champagne vinegar sounds indulgent, but it's very practical. Put leftover champagne in a bottle and add a dash of white vinegar 'mother' (the cloudy stuff at the bottom of a decent vinegar). Cork loosely and leave for a month, then filter into a clean bottle. Champagne vinegar is **excellent for vinaigrettes** and for perking up tomato salads.

47

Glaze a ham with bubbly.

Pop a cooked, smoked ham in a roasting tray. Pour over ½ bottle of sparkling wine and bake for 45 minutes at 180°C. Boil up another quarter of the bottle with a vanilla pod briefly, then stir in a cup of apple purée. Remove the pod and pour the mixture over the ham. Bake for another 45 minutes while drinking the rest of the bottle.

48

Wobbly bubbly!

To make champagne jelly,

stir together 2 tablespoons each of cold water and gelatine powder. Gently heat a cup of pink champagne to dissolve 150g (5oz) sugar. Away from the heat, whisk in the gelatine mix. Allow to cool and pour into 6 chilled glasses, topping up with champagne. Freeze for 20 minutes, then keep in the fridge.

49

Champagne granita is the best of all uses for leftover bubbly. Mix the wine respectfully with an equal amount of freshly squeezed orange juice, sugar to taste and a dash of fresh lime juice. Pour into a plastic tub and put in the freezer. Give it a stir after one hour, then put back and leave till needed.

50

Finally, here's **the most flamboyant way of opening a champagne bottle.** It is known as 'sabrage', because you use a cavalry sabre for the job. Holding the bottle in one hand, run the blunt edge of the sabre smartly up the glass so that it snaps off the neck at the little bulge called the 'collar'. Check for bottle fragments in your glass!

Andrew Langley

Andrew Langley is a knowledgeable food and drink writer. Among his formative influences he lists a season picking grapes in Bordeaux, several years of raising sheep and chickens in Wiltshire and two decades drinking his grandmother's tea. He has written books on a number of Scottish and Irish whisky distilleries and is the editor of the highly regarded anthology of the writings of the legendary Victorian chef Alexis Soyer.

THE LITTLE BOOK OF
BARBECUE
TIPS
ANDREW LANGLEY

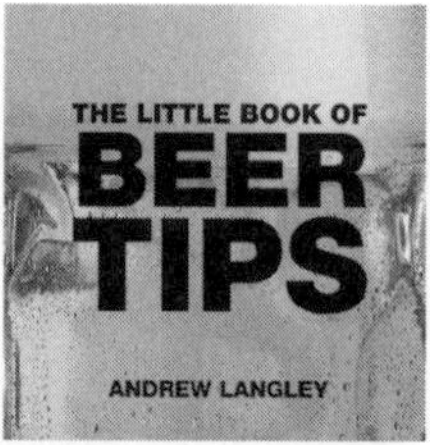
THE LITTLE BOOK OF
BEER
TIPS
ANDREW LANGLEY

THE LITTLE BOOK OF
HERB
TIPS
WILLIAM FORTT

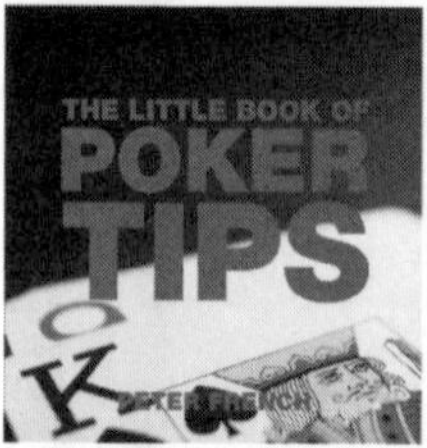
THE LITTLE BOOK OF
POKER
TIPS
PETER FRENCH

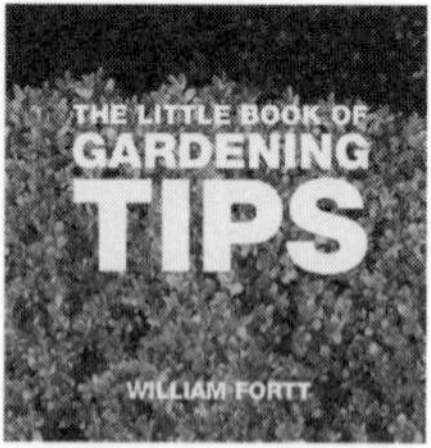
THE LITTLE BOOK OF
GARDENING
TIPS
WILLIAM FORTT

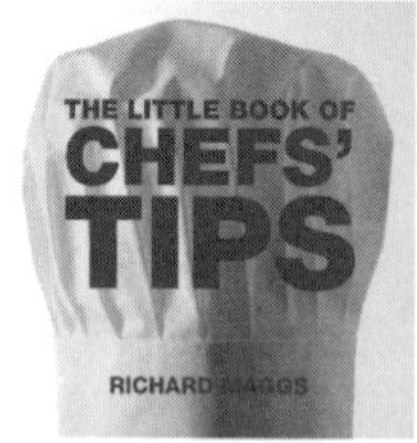
THE LITTLE BOOK OF
CHEFS'
TIPS
RICHARD MAGGS

THE LITTLE BOOK OF
SPICE
TIPS
ANDREW LANGLEY

THE LITTLE BOOK OF
GOLF
TIPS
PETER FRENCH

THE LITTLE BOOK OF
TIPS
SERIES

THE LITTLE BOOK OF
CHEESE
TIPS
ANDREW LANGLEY

THE LITTLE BOOK OF
WINE
TIPS
ANDREW LANGLEY

THE LITTLE BOOK OF
AGA
TIPS 2
RICHARD MAGGS

THE LITTLE BOOK OF
COFFEE
TIPS
ANDREW LANGLEY

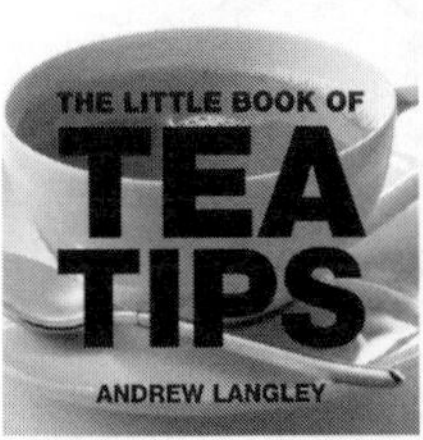
THE LITTLE BOOK OF
TEA
TIPS
ANDREW LANGLEY

THE LITTLE BOOK OF
AGA
TIPS 3
RICHARD MAGGS

THE LITTLE BOOK OF
AGA
TIPS
RICHARD MAGGS

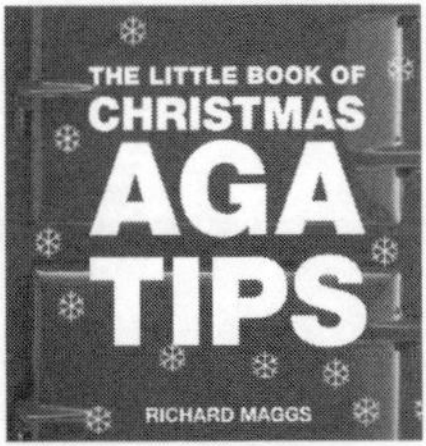
THE LITTLE BOOK OF
CHRISTMAS
AGA
TIPS
RICHARD MAGGS

THE LITTLE BOOK OF
RAYBURN
TIPS
RICHARD MAGGS

THE LITTLE BOOK OF
BRIDGE
TIPS
PETER FRENCH

THE LITTLE BOOK OF
CHESS
TIPS
PETER FRENCH

THE LITTLE BOOK OF
FISHING
TIPS
MICK DEVENISH

THE LITTLE BOOK OF
GREEN
TIPS
WILLIAM FORTT

THE LITTLE BOOK OF
KITTEN
TIPS
ANDREW LANGLEY

MARMITE
PAUL HARTLEY
THE LITTLE BOOK OF
MARMITE
TIPS

THE LITTLE BOOK OF
PUPPY
TIPS
ANDREW LANGLEY

THE LITTLE BOOK OF
WHISKY
TIPS
ANDREW LANGLEY
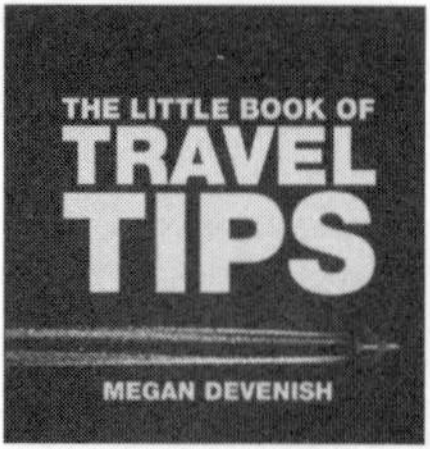
THE LITTLE BOOK OF
TRAVEL
TIPS
MEGAN DEVENISH

Little Books of Tips from Absolute Press

Aga Tips
Aga Tips 2
Aga Tips 3
Allotment Tips
Backgammon Tips
Barbecue Tips
Beer Tips
Bread Tips
Bread Machine Tips
Bridge Tips
Cake Baking Tips
Cake Decorating Tips
Champagne Tips
Cheese Tips
Chefs' Tips
Chess Tips
Chocolate Tips
Christmas Aga Tips
Chutney and Pickle Tips
Cocktail Tips
Coffee Tips
Cupcake Tips
Curry Tips
Fishing Tips
Fly Fishing Tips
Frugal Tips
Gardening Tips
Golf Tips
Green Tips
Grow Your Own Tips
Herb Tips
Houseplant Tips
Ice Cream Tips
Jam Tips
Kitten Tips
Macaroon Tips
Marmite Tips
Olive Oil Tips
Pasta Tips
Poker Tips
Puppy Tips
Rayburn Tips
Slow Cooker Tips
Spice Tips
Tea Tips
Travel Tips
Whisky Tips
Wine Tips
Wok Tips
Vinegar Tips